T0130290

The River Nile Frog Deceived The Nile Hare

Faustino Yacobo

Illustrated by
Edgin Santos

Copyright © 2009 by Faustino Yacobo. 563341

All rights reserved. No part of this book may be reproduced
or transmitted in any form or by any means, electronic or
mechanical, including photocopying, recording, or by any
information storage and retrieval system, without permission in
writing from the copyright owner.

To order additional copies of this book, contact:
Xlibris
1-888-795-4274
www.Xlibris.com
Orders@Xlibris.com

ISBN: Softcover   978-1-4363-9558-8
         EBook   978-1-7960-8432-0

Print information available on the last page

Rev. date: 01/22/2020

Dedication

This story is dedicated to my Daughter Reta Yacobo, my son, Zaiko Yacobo and to all my family and friends. This book would not have been possible without their support. My special thanks to Charles Yacobo, Morris Wande, Everett Minga, Charles Alcon, Gerry Spotts, Denis Lasuba, Robert Simbe, Jimmy Okot, Sabit Alley, Charity Kiden, and Sabiri Tambo. Also, I want to thank our late brother Stephen Amule Tambo with his great love for us when we were in Ifo refugee camp in Kenya. And, Edgin Santos for helping and giving me moral support during the hard time that I was going through, which led to the idea of writing this book.

Introduction

The River Nile Frogs Deceived The Nile Hare: is a fictitious story told to me by my grandmother when I was a small boy in Southern Sudan. The story teaches and encourages children to ask for help when they are in trouble. Children often learn from their parents and when parents lie, their Children also lie. Many parents often make the mistake of lying in front of their children when cornered by thinking that children duplicate what their parents teach.

Do you ever wonder why some parents are angry when their children lie at them and ask where the children learned to lie? Parents who care provide clear rules for your children and also give them lots of love within the house. Set a good example for your children so they can learn from watching you and try to understand what your children need not lying to them. This book tells a simple kid's story about a lie that got a Frog called Karaba into trouble and asking for help when in trouble.

Once upon a time, a thirsty Hare called Likambo, went to the bank
of River Nile to drink a water. At the bank of the Nile River, after
drinking water, Likambo spent some good time at the River Nile bank.

Likambo, saw a Frog jumping from one corner of the bank to another. Likambo, was surprised and wondered and then said to the Frog, I am sorry to disturb you. Do you mind if I ask you some questions? I am called Likambo, and what is your name? My name is Karaba. Why can't you walk or run instead of jumping? Suppose an enemy attacked you, is this how you are going to save yourself by jumping from one spot to another? Karaba said to Mr. Likambo, this is just for fun; I can walk and run faster than you.

Mr. Likambo could not believe what Mr. Karaba just said and asked, are you saying that you can run faster than me? Yes, the Karaba replied, I will run faster than you, Likambo.

Okay Karaba, I am going to issue you a challenge to race me. Why can't we meet next week, on Friday, at 7:30 a.m. in the same place so that we can race? I am going to give you one week to think about it. If you change your mind and decide not to race me because you know you won't win let me know. Mr. Karaba said, deal. Let's do it next week, I am ready to bet you.

What did my big mouth got myself into, Karaba thought to himself after, Likambo left. I know I can't run and certainly can't win a race with Likambo! What can I do to win this race, Karaba asked himself. I am in a big trouble, big trouble, big trouble, he repeated.

All of a sudden Karaba, saw other frog in the middle of the Nile River. Excuse me my friend, Karaba said to the other Frog! I am in big trouble and I need your help. What can I do for you, one of the Frogs asked? I lied to Likambo that I can run and now Likambo issued a challenge for me to race him next week. I now don't know what to do! I have no way out but to ask you my friend for help. Who is Likambo? Is Likambo a Hare? Oh! First of all where are you from? What is your name? I am Karaba. And you? I am called Clay from the River Nile. He answered, I am from the River Nile too! You know that you can't run Karaba, we all can't run, why then do you want to lie like that to Likambo? Me and my big mouth got me into this trouble, Karaba replied.

Mr. Clay, said you know my friend; there is a solution to any problems. Since we all are frogs from the River Nile, we will be willing to help you, but, you will have to promise us not to lie again. We don't usually help frogs that lie and we don't allow them among us. I have learned my lesson and will not lie again, Karaba promised. Mr. Clay I will pass this message to our Leader called Waledyei. I hope he will come to the meeting and pass this message to all the frogs to help you. The Leader Mr. Waledyei got the message and said okay. Okay, we are going to have a secret meeting to come up with a plan to win this race against Likambo. Mr. Waledyei said. First, we must send a message to all the Frogs along the Nile to come altogether for a meeting; beginning from Lake Victoria all the way to the Mediterranean Sea.

I wish I am like that big bird by the Nile river bank.

You are a Frog not a bird why do you want to be a bird?

So I can fly to win the race against Likambo.

Discipline yourself by doing what is right not what is wrong.

Remember when you keep on lying you are hurting yourself, and no one will ever believe you.

It is good that you asked for help and I am willing to help you Karaba.

Do not repeat the same mistake again.

Let us send the message to all the Nile River Frogs to come together for the meeting.

The message went out and the Frogs came for the meeting.

My friends first of all I want to thank each of you for coming to this meeting. My name is called Waledyei for those of you who do not hear of me and know me.

If we don't win this race against Likambo we will all be losers, the Leader of the frogs said in the meeting. We all are winners in this room and have never lost to anyone before.

We have to work together as one family, a third frog agreed. Together we will be stronger and win this race. My brothers, and sisters, do not worry, we are going to win this race if we work together with one mind and one understanding. Together we will win.

What is the secret plan, Mr. Clay asked in the meeting?

The leader replied, the plan is to line up all the Frogs of the River Nile along the line from the start of the race to the end. Because we are smaller than Likambo and he will not be able to see us during the race. So, when Likambo call out where are you Mr. Karaba the Frog close to Likambo will answer, I am here close to you. We will continue to say this until the last frog at the finish line.

So the message went out to all the Frogs along the River Nile including those who did not attend the meeting.

This meeting is dismissed. Everybody run for your life there is a big snake coming.

Run for your life.

Thank you all for coming to this last meeting, Waledyei said. And thank you for running away from the big snake.

I am so happy to see your beautiful faces all here today.

I am glad that we can come together to help one of our brothers, Karaba.

Let us now go out there and win this race, because we all are winners.

On the day of the race all the frogs are lined up on the race line.

Likambo was already at the start line getting ready for the race.

Likambo, said to Karaba you know I am going to beat you and I am feeling a winner already.

Let us start the race and see who the loser is going to be, Karaba replied.

The race was on time Likambo and Karaba were there at the start of the line. After a few minutes the race started and Likambo, ran very faster while all the frogs are line up.

Likambo call out where are you Karaba the frog that is close, answered I am here and I don't see you running with me Likambo said. I am running behind you, one of the frogs in the line answered.

Likambo was encouraged to hear that Karaba is behind him and he continues to run.

Again after some hours Likambo call out, where are you Karaba. I can't see you. The next frog in the line replied, I can see you and I'm here in front of you.

If you run faster, you will see me. Likambo, is surprised that Karaba is now in front of him, he therefore increased his speed with the hope to see Karaba.

All long the race whenever Likambo called out where are you, the next Frog, in the line replies, I can see you and I am here in front of you.

Likambo continues to run faster and faster. Likambo, did all the running and all the frogs replied the same whenever Likambo, called out where are you Karaba.

Finally, closing to the finish line, Likambo called out one more time, stop playing Karaba, where are you? I see you running close to the finish line and I am already here in the finish line.

The last Frog answered. After reaching the finish line, Likambo, asked, how did you do it Karaba?

I told you from the beginning that I am going to win this race, but you didn't believe me. Maybe, now is the time you start believing again. I am from the River Nile my friend, we run faster.

After Likambo, left and was mad, Karaba, went back to his friends and thanked the leader of the Frogs Waledyei, and all the frogs for helping him win the race against Mr. Likambo. All the Frogs went back home happy that they won.

The author and his daughter

Printed in the United States
By Bookmasters